D1613649

# OLD-TIME SILHOUETTES

Compiled and Arranged by

## Judy M. Johnson

DOVER PUBLICATIONS, INC.

New York

*My thanks to my grandmother, Sylvia Heath, for sharing her collection of paper treasures, and to my mother, Helen Johnson, who also gathered silhouettes for me to add to this collection.*

*Bibliographical Note*

*Old-Time Silhouettes* is a new work, first published by Dover Publications, Inc., in 1994.

DOVER *Pictorial Archive* SERIES

This book belongs to the Dover Pictorial Archive Series. You may use the designs and illustrations for graphics and crafts applications, free and without special permission, provided that you include no more than ten in the same publication or project. (For permission for additional use, please write to Dover Publications, Inc., 180 Varick St., New York, N.Y. 10014.)

However, republication or reproduction of any illustration by any other graphic service whether it be in a book or in any other design resource is strictly prohibited.

*Library of Congress Cataloging-in-Publication Data*

Old-time silhouettes / compiled and arranged by Judy M. Johnson.
    p.    cm. — (Dover pictorial archive series)
    ISBN 0-486-27940-5 (pbk.)
    1. Silhouettes.  I. Johnson, Judy M.  II. Series.
NC910.042  1994
745.4—dc20
                                     93–45545
                                         CIP

Manufactured in the United States of America
Dover Publications, Inc., 31 East 2nd Street, Mineola, N.Y. 11501

# Publisher's Note

The controller-general of France from March to November 1759, Etienne de Silhouette, was a frugal man who kept himself entertained by cutting portraits in paper. Such work gradually became known as *portraits à la Silhouette*. In the western world, at least, this term stuck, and the Frenchman left his name to an art form whose tradition stretched at least as far back as the Tang Dynasty in China (A.D. 618–907) and whose essential principle would, within the next hundred years, provide the basis of photography as we know it. At any rate, these works in light and darkness remain popular for their unique ability to play in simple forms and to show in shadows the hidden drama of the quotidian.

In this anthology from the 1920s and 1930s, the images come from techniques as varied as classic scissor-cut, pen and ink, woodcut and halftone. Some use the ingenious method of having portions of the design, usually human limbs, disappear into a white background, leaving only the black of the costume to help the mind fill in the blanks. In addition, designs are included that originally appeared in old children's magazines, and were meant to be cut out for creative play. Modern photocopying will of course facilitate this use of the *entire* book, not just the children's section.

However this volume is used—whether as a source of illustration or a picture book to be browsed through—it is a treasure of classic design in an old-fashioned mode.

# Contents

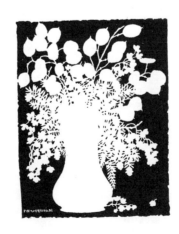

Before (Baby Comes)

A SELLER OF PLASTER IMAGES

# SHADOW-PICTURE

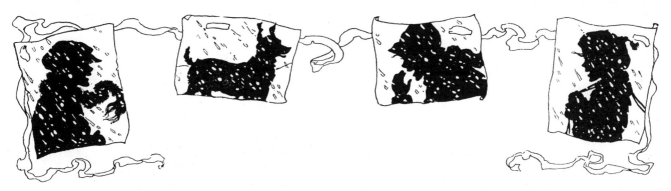

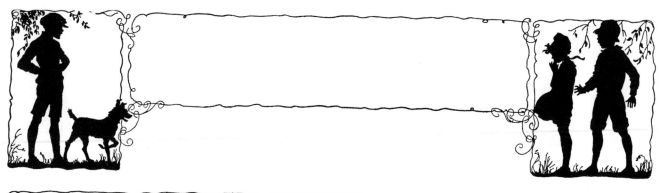

Washington's Coach

A VALENTINE PARTY

# THE OLD LION

APPLE HILL FARMS
H. WARD Prop.

FRESH PICKED
VEGATABLES
HONEY
PEACHES—
30¢ Basket

THE DANCE

# Something To Do For Girls

# Something To Do For Boys

Around the deep, dark water,
Oh, children, have a care;
Unless you are good swimmers,
You never should play there.

Now, don't you bark or whimper, Punch!
   The fish are swimming round my spinner,
And soon we'll catch a bass for lunch
   And half a dozen perch for dinner.

The puppy found a woodchuck hole;
   I found a spotted partridge feather;
We crossed the brook, we climbed the knoll,
   And both came running home together.

*Verses by* ARTHUR GUITERMAN

Two long-eared rabbits live below
   The wall around my little garden;
Perhaps they eat a leaf or so,
   But when they do they beg my pardon.

The wild canary preens his wing;
   He turns his head and keeps it bobbing;
And then you ought to hear him sing
   And watch his throat go throbbing, throbbing!

Little children, do not
play
In the street on any day,
For trucks and horses,
street cars, too,
May very badly injure
you.

44     Children

54    Kitchen Chores

FEED
ME

PENGUINS

MARSH BIRDS

DECORATION BY HELENE NYCE

Cooperation is better than conflict